Cornerstones of Freedom

The Story of

THE SPIRIT OF ST. LOUIS

By. R. Conrad Stein

Illustrated by Len Meents

 CHILDRENS PRESS, CHICAGO

Library of Congress Cataloging in Publication Data

Stein, R. Conrad.
  The story of the Spirit of St. Louis.

  (Cornerstones of Freedom)
  Summary: Describes the celebrated 1927 New York-to-
Paris flight of Charles A. Lindbergh, which was the
first transatlantic solo flight in history, as well as
the first non-stop flight between the two cities.
  1. Lindbergh, Charles, 1902-1974—Juvenile literature.   2. Transatlantic flights—Juvenile literature.
3. Air pilots—United States—Biography—Juvenile literature. [1. Lindbergh, Charles, 1902-1974. 2. Transatlantic flights. 3. Air pilots. 4. Aeronautics—His-
tory] I. Meents, Len W., ill. II. Title.
TL540.L5S73 1984   629.13'092'4 [B] [92]   83-23174
ISBN 0-516-04667-5

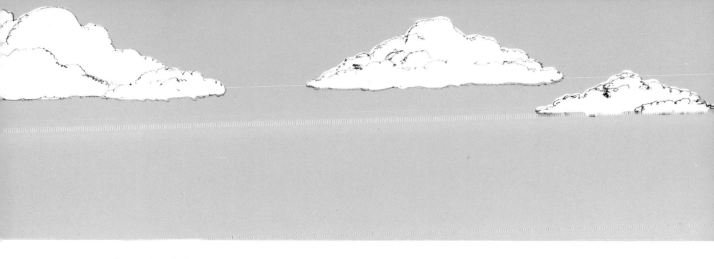

Paris, France.   May 8, 1927.   5:00 A.M.

At Le Bourget Airfield, an excited crowd gathered hoping to witness history in the making. Two French aviators were about to climb into the sky and try to fly nonstop to New York. Piloting the airplane was a World War I ace named Charles Nungesser. Another experienced airman named Francois Coli served as navigator.

The crowd fell silent as the buzz of the single engine became a roar. Slowly the plane bumped along the runway. Sitting in the open cockpit, pilot Nungesser shouted to the crowd. His words were drowned out by the screaming engine, but the spectators could read his lips: *"Au revoir. Au revoir."* ("Good-bye. Good-bye.") Loaded down with almost nine hundred gallons of gasoline, the plane stubbornly resisted takeoff. Nungesser kept the throttle at full speed, rolling the aircraft faster, faster, faster. Finally, after the plane had exhausted almost a mile of runway, the wheels left the ground.

Nungesser buzzed over the field and saw people waving handkerchiefs, waving hats, waving tiny French flags. Then the plane became a dot disappearing over the western horizon. The world held its breath wondering if these two Frenchmen would complete their mission.

At first, the flight progressed exactly according to schedule. An hour and a half after takeoff, Nungesser and Coli's airplane was seen crossing the English Channel. Five hours later, it was spotted near the coast of Ireland. French men and women slept fitfully that night. Their thoughts and prayers were locked on the flight of their two countrymen. Then, at 10:00 A.M. Paris time, the French radio announced that the plane had been seen in the skies above Newfoundland, Canada. The heroes had made it across the Atlantic Ocean!

Further radio reports came in. The plane had been seen over Portland, Maine. It had been spotted above Boston. Finally, an extra edition of the newspaper *La Presse* hit the streets of Paris. It bore a screaming headline that said Nungesser and Coli had landed in New York City to the cheers of thousands of Americans. All of France went wild.

But no such landing had taken place. Later, an

embarrased official of the newspaper admitted they
had fabricated the story to get the jump on other
papers. The sightings over Maine and Boston also
seemed to be fabrications.

Hours passed. Too many hours. Nungesser and
Coli's plane had used up all its fuel, yet there was no
sign of the two Frenchmen. The United States Navy
began a massive search. But neither the bodies of
the aviators nor the wreckage of the plane was
found. The aircraft had crashed either in the freezing waters of the Atlantic or in the wilds of Newfoundland.

Two more men had died trying to fly between New York and Paris. In 1919, a French millionaire had offered a $25,000 prize to the first pilot or crew to fly nonstop between the two cities. Nungesser and Coli were the fifth and sixth airmen to lose their lives attempting the flight.

While the world mourned the loss of the two Frenchmen, an American pilot readied his airplane to attempt the Paris flight. He was a quiet, shy, twenty-five-year-old bachelor named Charles Augustus Lindbergh. Unlike other pilots competing for the prize money, Lindbergh was not a famous aviator. But he was tough, intelligent, and perhaps the best pilot in America.

Aviation was just a quarter of a century old at the time Lindbergh and others attempted the jump between continents. In 1903, Orville and Wilbur Wright had launched a new era when their flying machine struggled into the air at a hill near Kitty Hawk, North Carolina.

Soon after the Wright brothers' flight, other flying machines appeared. Those early aircraft were little more than motorized kites. They were built on frames made of sticks, held together with baling wire, covered with muslin cloth, and driven by engines about as powerful as those on today's lawn mowers.

Still, those fragile machines took up the challenge of conquering distance. Flying became a contest pitting men against natural barriers. In 1909, a Frenchman named Louis Blériot became the first man to fly across the English Channel. Crossing the twenty-three-mile channel took the French pilot thirty-six minutes. In 1910, a Peruvian flyer, Jorge Chávez, became the first aviator to fly over the Alps. He crashed and died, and his last words were, "Higher, ever higher." In 1913, a Frenchman named Roland Garros crossed the Mediterranean Sea. His plane carried enough fuel for an eight-hour flight.

The trip lasted seven hours and fifty-three minutes.
In the United States, too, natural barriers tumbled
as pilots flew over the Allegheny Mountains, over
the Rocky Mountains, over parts of the Great Lakes.

World War I put an end to the marathon distance
flights. But during the war, aircraft design
improved tremendously. When peace came, aviators
dreamed of overcoming the greatest of all natural
barriers—the Atlantic Ocean.

In the skies above the Atlantic, pilots had to fly
into the teeth of gales that could slow their aircraft
almost to a walk. They had to push through clouds of
freezing mist that coated the wings with ice. Finally, the immense size of the ocean staggered the
minds of pilots. Even at its shortest point, between

Newfoundland and Ireland, the Atlantic Ocean stretched some nineteen hundred miles.

In June, 1919, two British airmen named John Alcock and Whitten Brown climbed aboard a fragile-looking double-engined biplane. They took off from a cow pasture in Newfoundland and headed out to sea. Sixteen hours later, they crash-landed in a marsh on the coast of Ireland. Their voyage had been perilous, but their achievement incredible. Midway across the Atlantic, they almost plunged into the water while lost in an ice cloud. Near the Irish coast, one of their engines began sputtering, and they were running dangerously low on fuel. Yet history records the Englishmen Alcock and Brown as the first to fly nonstop across the Atlantic Ocean.

But aviators dreamed of doing more than merely crossing the Atlantic at its narrowest stretch. They wanted to fly from a city in the New World to a city in the Old World or vice versa. When the $25,000 prize was offered, the New York-to-Paris flight became an obsession among airmen of the 1920s.

On a misty morning at Roosevelt Field, New York, Charles Lindbergh revved his engine. The date was May 20, 1927. Because some St. Louis businessmen had helped him to buy his plane, Lindbergh named the craft *Spirit of St. Louis.* Unlike the previous planes to attempt the flight, his was a single seater. To save weight, Lindbergh had decided to fly solo.

From takeoff to landing, Lindbergh's voyage spanned 3,600 miles. For a 1927 aircraft, that was almost the equivalent of flying from the earth to the moon today. The *Spirit of St. Louis* was loaded down with gasoline—514 gallons, to be exact. Carrying that much fuel made the plane weigh 5,135 pounds, which was slightly more than the wings were designed to carry. Complicating matters, rain had fallen the night before and the aircraft wheels sank to the axles in mire.

At 7:45 A.M., Lindbergh told his ground crew he was ready. A crowd gathered to cheer the takeoff. Slowly, almost painfully, the aircraft rolled forward. "The *Spirit of St. Louis* feels more like a truck than

an airplane," Lindbergh wrote later. Far in front of him stood a line of telephone poles with wires strung between them. As the engine roared, the plane bumped up to the speed of thirty, then forty miles per hour. Suddenly, the telephone poles loomed dangerously close. There was not enough runway left to stop even if Lindbergh had wanted to. The straining engine seemed to be shaking the aircraft to pieces. Water and mud splattered against the bottoms of the wings. Finally, Lindbergh felt the plane's weight shift from wheels to wings. He had made it into the air, just barely clearing the telephone lines.

Steadily Lindbergh eased his aircraft into a cruising altitude. Then he slouched in his seat and thought of the many hours and miles that lay ahead of him. His only provisions consisted of five sandwiches and a quart of water. Regarding food, Lindbergh had told a member of his ground crew, "If I get to Paris I won't need any more. If I don't get to Paris I won't need any more either."

Charles Augustus Lindbergh was born on February 4, 1902, in Detroit, Michigan. He grew up on a farm in Minnesota. His father was a lawyer who later became a United States congressman. His mother taught high school chemistry. Despite having gifted parents, Lindbergh was a poor student. However, he showed flashes of brilliance in math, and had a marvelous mechanical ability. He was able to fix any kind of motor regardless of its condition.

While a boy on his parents' farm, Charles heard a buzzing in the sky and looked up to see an airplane soaring through the clouds. A chilling feeling swept over him. He knew his destiny would be in the skies. For the rest of his life, aviation became like a religion to him. He later wrote that long, lonely flights enabled him to commune with ghosts and guardian spirits.

Lindbergh attended the University of Wisconsin for two years, but dropped out to enroll in a flight school. There, the once poor student finished first in his class. Upon receiving his pilot's license, Lindbergh took up barnstorming. Barnstormers were daredevil pilots who performed stunts at carnivals and fairs. Often one barnstormer flew an airplane while another boldly walked along the top of a wing. Lindbergh wing walked several times, and later said it wasn't as dangerous as it looked to the people on the ground.

After barnstorming for two years, Lindbergh became a flier for the United States Air Mail Service. Flying the mail in the 1920s was a job for skilled aviators only. Lindbergh and others had to fly great distances in nasty weather. During those long flights, Lindbergh's ears were attuned to even the smallest change in the purr of the motor. "Let a cylinder miss once," he wrote, "and I'll feel it as clearly as though a human heart had skipped against my thumb."

Lindbergh was also a gifted writer. Twenty-five years after his epic flight, he wrote a book called *The Spirit of St. Louis.* It gave a chilling hour-by-hour account of his lonely flight over the mighty

Atlantic. He wrote the book largely in the present tense, so it reads like an event happening at the moment.

"I'm alone at last, over the first short stretch of sea on the route to France," Lindbergh wrote about his feelings while crossing the shoreline. "It's only 35 miles to the Connecticut shore, but I've never flown across that much water before." Flying over water was Lindbergh's only weakness as a pilot. The midwesterner had never before ventured near an ocean in his plane. But he knew the dangers of ice clouds—those massive gray pillows in the air that seemed to prowl the Atlantic like beasts on the hunt. In his book he described ice clouds with a feeling of terror only a pilot could express. "They enmesh intruders. They're barbaric in their methods. They toss you in their inner turbulence, lash you with their hailstones, poison you with freezing mist."

The immensity of the ocean suddenly overwhelmed Lindbergh. His flight was only an hour old, but already he began to have doubts about its success. "Looking ahead at the unbroken horizon and limitless expanse of water, I'm struck by my arrogance in attempting such a flight. I'm giving up a continent and heading out to sea in the most fragile vehicle ever devised by man. . . . Why have I dared stake my life on the belief. . . that I can find my way through shifting air to Europe?"

But gradually the ocean looked less forbidding. He dropped down until his wheels were skimming just six feet above the water's surface. "The *Spirit of St. Louis* is like a butterfly blown out to sea. How often I used to watch [butterflies], as a child, on the banks of the Mississippi, dancing up and down above the water, as I am doing now. . . . But a touch of wing to water, and they were down forever, just as my plane would be. Why, I used to wonder, did [the butterflies] ever leave the safety of land? But why have I? How similar my position has become."

19

Soaring above the waves, the *Spirit of St. Louis* looked like a delicate silver toy. Lindbergh had helped to design the plane. It was twenty-eight feet long with a wingspan of forty-six feet. This made it a small aircraft even by 1927 standards. It was powered by a newly designed engine that had nine cylinders jutting out of a single crankcase like the spokes of a wheel. The lightweight engine was unusually powerful. To save weight, Lindbergh had refused to carry a radio, and had even refused to take a parachute. Yet the *Spirit of St. Louis* was so loaded with fuel that the motor could manage an air speed of only 102 miles per hour.

During his fourth hour aloft, Lindbergh remembered that his last night on the ground had been sleepless. "It would be pleasant to doze off a few seconds. But I mustn't feel sleepy at this stage of the trip! Why I'm less than a tenth of the way to Paris. . . . " He also noticed a clump of mud that had plastered itself onto the bottom of one of his wings during takeoff. "I want to reach out and scrape it off. . . but it's an arm's length too far away. Why should I have to carry its extra weight and resistance all the way across the ocean?" He knew those few ounces of mud could not slow the plane down more than a fraction of a mile an hour. "But when one is tired, small items draw undue attention." As the trip progressed, that wretched clump of mud clinging to the bottom of his wing drove Lindbergh nearly crazy.

Lindbergh flew a northerly circular course designed to take him back over land once more before his final ocean crossing. The fifth hour found him flying over the wilds of Nova Scotia in Canada. The need for sleep still gripped him. He stuck a hand out the window and tried to scoop cold air against his face in the hope it would wake him up. Luckily, his engine still throbbed a steady beat. He risked burning extra fuel to buzz over the town of St. John's, Newfoundland. Townspeople waved up at him. Then he banked his plane over the Atlantic, pointing the nose toward the coast of Ireland almost two thousand miles away. "The last gate is closing behind me."

Ships avoided the northerly route Lindbergh had chosen. The pilot quickly understood why. Suddenly, shockingly, he realized he had entered the menacing realm of the Arctic. Below him sprawled a huge ice field that looked like a frozen desert. "As far as I can see ahead, the ocean is glaring white. . . . I feel surrounded by the stillness of [it]—the frozen silence of the north. I feel a trespasser in forbidden latitudes, in air where such a little plane and I have no authority to be."

Night fell like the blow of a hammer. Fog blanketed the airplane. The luminous dials of the instrument panel stared up at Lindbergh with ghostlike eyes. His life depended on the compass needle. If his compass failed, or if he erred in reading it, he might fly in endless circles above the Atlantic until he ran out of gas.

In the blackness, Lindbergh suddenly felt his plane's wings shudder. The *Spirit of St. Louis* shook as if caught in the fist of an angry giant. Wondering what was going on outside, Lindbergh found his flashlight and played the beam along a wing. *Ice!* Because of the fog, he had flown blindly into an ice cloud. These were the same dreaded monsters he had so hoped to avoid.

"I've got to turn around, get back into clear air— quickly!" But if he jerked his rudder, he could lose control of his aircraft in the wild currents. Telling himself to be calm, Lindbergh began a long, lazy turn. His eyes locked on the instrument panel. Already he had lost ten miles per hour in air speed

and a hundred feet in altitude. This was caused by the crust of ice growing on the wings. The longer he remained in the clouds, the thicker the coating of ice would become. Still, Lindbergh continued his gradual turn. One fast move could mean a fatal plunge into the sea.

Then, finally, "My eyes sense a change in the blackness of my cockpit. I look out the window. Can those be the same stars? Is this the same sky? How bright! How clear! What safety I have reached."

After waiting a few minutes, Lindbergh turned his flashlight on the wings once more. The ice was receding. But somehow that stubborn clump of mud remained cemented on his wing. He cursed it.

In the starlit night, Lindbergh discovered that he was surrounded by ice clouds. Their gray shapes rose out of the Atlantic like giant inverted icicles. "Great cliffs tower over me, ward me off with icy walls. They belong to mountains of another world. . . . To plunge into these mountains of the heavens would be like stepping into quicksand." He pressed on, weaving between the ice clouds much like a hiker in mountain country threads through valleys.

During his nineteenth hour in the air, Lindbergh reached the point of no return. He no longer had enough fuel to turn back to America. He would either land in Europe or crash into the sea. "I've burned my last bridge behind me."

Sleep. How delicious it would be to catch just five minutes of sleep. But Lindbergh knew that if he dozed off for even a few seconds, he would be likely to wake up in a spinning dive he could never pull out of. He stamped his feet. He stretched his neck to put his face into the slipstream outside. He shouted in the cockpit at the top of his lungs. Anything to fight off dozing. But the steady drone of the engine sounded like a dangerous lullaby. "I'm passing out. . . . Can I hold onto consciousness?

He took a long drink from his icy water bottle. Five drowsy minutes passed. Suddenly, miraculously, he snapped out of his sleepiness. It was as if his tortured body had passed through some magic curtain. The change he felt was mystical. "Am I crossing the bridge which one sees only in his last, departing moments? Am I already beyond the point from which I can bring my vision back to earth and men? Death no longer seems the final end it used to be."

To the east, the sun inched over the horizon. The pilot saw long fingers of red stretching into the sky. He had survived the ordeal of a night alone over the Atlantic.

Lindbergh flew as if he were in a trance. Although no longer sleepy, he felt somehow unreal. He thought he saw islands jutting out of the blue water, but he knew land was still many hours away. At one point, he believed he had company in his tiny plane. "The fusilage behind me becomes filled with ghostly presences. . . . These phantoms speak with human voices, conversing and advising me on my flight, discussing problems of my navigation, reassuring me."

His twenty-seventh hour aloft found Lindbergh dreamily buzzing over the waves when he saw a curious white speck in the water. Were his eyes still playing tricks? No, there was another one. Fishing boats! This meant that the coast of Ireland had to be near.

Lindbergh slowed his engine to a soft throb. His plane glided inches above one of the boats' sails.

"Hey, where's Ireland?" the pilot shouted to the fishermen. "Which way is Ireland?"

A shocked fisherman poked his head out of a porthole. He stared at the tiny airplane as if he were frozen. The man neither waved nor uttered a word.

This kind of greeting from the first human face he saw on the other side of the world annoyed Lindbergh. He remembered a line from a poem. "These boats remind me of the 'painted ship upon a painted ocean.'"

An hour later, Lindbergh spotted land. This time it was no hallucination. First he saw a few rocks in the mist. Then a coastline. Ireland! Roaring over the shoreline, Lindbergh became the first man to fly the Atlantic alone.

Wide awake now, Lindbergh soared over Ireland and the southern tip of England. Below, people waved at his tiny silver plane. In turn, Lindbergh banked his wings. Unknown to Lindbergh, radios sang the news to the entire world: "He did it. That crazy Yank did it. He made it across the Atlantic!"

Night fell again, but the skies were clear. Lindbergh saw streetlights and automobile lights burning below before he crossed the English channel. Over France, he followed the River Seine. Ahead, a huge patch of light glowed like a distant fire—Paris. He had endured thirty-three hours in the air. Now, strangely, he regretted that it was all over. In the center of the brightly lighted avenues of Paris, Lindbergh spotted the Eiffel Tower. He circled it once, found his field, and landed. Then all of Paris found him.

A crowd of thousands poured onto the airfield to greet the American. People pulled Lindbergh out of his cockpit and passed him overhead hand to hand. Luckily, two French aviators rescued Lindbergh and hurried him to a hangar. But the celebration continued. He came home to a New York ticker-tape parade that has never been equaled. The *New York Times* devoted its first sixteen pages to stories about him and his flight. He was called the "Lone Eagle" and "Lucky Lindy."

Lindbergh, an intensely private man, hoped his sudden fame would quickly fade. But for years afterward he was such a popular figure that people stole his dirty laundry just for souvenirs. "I've had enough fame for a dozen lives," a disgusted Lindbergh once wrote. "It's not what it's cracked up to be."

Tragedy and controversy plagued Lindbergh after his flight. He was married in 1929. In 1932, his twenty-month old son was kidnapped and later found murdered. An unemployed carpenter named Bruno Hauptmann was executed for the crime. Newspapers sensationalized the murder, calling it "the crime of the century." Reporters ignored the Lindberghs' grief and nagged the couple for interviews. Two incredibly tasteless photographers broke into the Trenton, New Jersey, morgue to take pictures of the murdered boy's body. The Lindberghs moved to Europe to seek peace.

In Europe, Lindbergh admired Nazi Germany's aviation industry. He also became an active member of a movement that hoped to keep the United States out of the war that seemed to be brewing in the Old World. Finally, he accepted a Medal of Honor presented to him by the head of the German Air Force, Hermann Goering. Critics charged that he was anti-American, anti-Jewish, and anti-British. He hotly denied all charges.

After World War II, Lindbergh finally faded from the public spotlight. He remained in the aviation industry and helped to design aircraft. He was one of the designers of today's Boeing 747 jumbo jet. In the 1960s he spoke out for conservation of the nation's forests and against the killing of whales. Lindbergh died at his home in Hawaii on August 26, 1974.

The *Spirit of St. Louis* now hangs in the National Air and Space Museum in Washington, D.C. The museum is part of the Smithsonian Institution. Before his death, Lindbergh often visited the Smithsonian to gaze at the famous aircraft. He would pull his hat over his eyes so he wouldn't be

recognized. It is difficult to imagine his thoughts as he joined the throng of tourists crowding around his old plane. Lindbergh was far more than just a superb pilot. He was a curious mixture of mystic and mechanic, dreamer and engineer, technician and poet.

Above all, Lindbergh was a passionate believer in the wonders of science. But late in his life, he recognized that even science has its limits. He wrote, "It took me years to discover that science, with all its brilliance, lights only a middle chapter of creation. [It is] a chapter with both ends bordering on the infinite. One which can be forever expanded but never completed."

About the Author

R. Conrad Stein was born and grew up in Chicago. He enlisted in the Marine Corps at the age of eighteen, and served for three years. He then attended the University of Illinois, where he received a Bachelor of Arts degree in history. He later studied in Mexico and earned a Master of Fine Arts degree from the University of Guanajuato.

The study of history is Mr. Stein's hobby. Since he finds it to be an exciting subject, he tries to bring the excitement of history to his readers. He is the author of many other books, articles, and short stories written for young people.

Mr. Stein is married to Deborah Kent, who is also a writer of books for young readers.

About the Artist

Len Meents studied painting and drawing at Southern Illinois University and after graduation in 1969 he moved to Chicago. Mr. Meents works full time as a painter and illustrator. He and his wife and children currently make their home in LaGrange, Illinois.